Did You Know?

YOU ARE THE SHIT!

JEREMY CLARK

Copyright © 2021 Jeremy Clark

All rights reserved.

ISBN: 978-0-578-91632-3

DEDICATION

"I hate that word 'can't.'"

— Johnny B. Clark, my Father

I AM doing it Dad.

CONTENTS

	Introduction	1
1	What are affirmations?	3
2	Why do we have negative thoughts?	5
3	R&R—Recognition & Rejection	9
4	How to use affirmations	15
5	Ultra-Awareness State	21
6	Fulfillment Journal Purpose	22
7	Your Journey Starts Now	23
8	Affirmation List	224

INTRODUCTION

I wrote this book because I needed it.

You opened this book because you needed it.

Did you know that you are the shit?

WHAT ARE AFFIRMATIONS?

So you want to know what the big deal is with affirmations? Why are they so important? Simply put, affirmations can change the direction of your life within minutes or even seconds. Affirmations are short and powerful statements that can instantly change your mood by affecting your conscious and subconscious mind. We as humans have several hundreds of thousands of thoughts that run through our minds daily, and sadly for most humans, a majority of those thoughts are negative. Thankfully, these negative thoughts can be turned into positive thoughts.

Your happiness can be limitless, and your goals are closer than what they may seem to be right now. Once you change your mindset from a negative to a positive, you begin to attract your true desires, and by doing so distance yourself from the self-sabotaging thoughts that hinder your ability to reach your true calling. You will become the person you think you are, and it is important to know you are a person of high value.

Once you understand the power of positive affirmations and begin to implement them in your everyday life, watch how your life starts to change for the better. If you are truly looking to get over the hump, get out of your own way, and attract what you deserve, then these affirmations are for you. You must believe that you already have the tools necessary to achieve what you want out of life, and that starts within your mind.

Think of your life as a journey and your body as the vehicle. Your brain is the engine (or motor, if you drive an electric car smart ass). You tell me what kind of car can get to its destination without a functional engine or motor? I'll wait. Like a vehicle, you must perform routine maintenance on your mind to make sure you can get to your destination. Affirmations are the mind's maintenance that you need to get the body, your vehicle, to its destination. Remember, you are always in control of your vehicle when you are aware that you are driving it!

WHY DO WE HAVE NEGATIVE THOUGHTS?

We have negative thoughts because, to put it simply, it's easy. It's the easy way out to tell yourself that the goal you made for yourself is unattainable. The steps to reach your goal are too hard. It's easy to be by yourself and say, "I don't have the resources I need to make this happen." Well guess what? You probably never say any of these things out loud. The only time you most likely say these types of statements out loud is when you are around others, and you are expressing to them what you feel you can't do. Even in these situations it's more of a cry for help to the people you are talking to, to give you a direction on how to achieve your goal rather than a real feeling that you can't reach your goal. These self-debilitating thoughts cripple your body from proceeding with action towards your goals.

It's an inner battle within our brains between dopamine and cortisol. These two hormones feed our brains' reactive system, which determines what we feel to be right or wrong. To be exact, dopamine is a neurotransmitter or happy hormone that releases feelings of positivity in our minds. After achieving whatever we deem within ourselves to be an accomplishment, our brains release dopamine that communicates with the nerves in our body that make us feel good about what we have just experienced. Cortisol is a hormone that regulates your body's internal fight-or-flight system, like your immune response. However, cortisol is also our body's primary stress hormone that causes our minds to worry about what may or may not happen in our current or future situations. Our minds crave dopamine for our accomplishments and everyday interactions, but the cortisol hormone is more easily released due to uncertainty. This is because outcomes of our actions that we deem to be accomplishments can feel few and far between, and the time between can lead to a cortisol build-up of worries, doubts, and what-ifs about getting to the next accomplishment. These worries and doubts are negative fuel to our subconscious mind that hinders our ability to visualize where we are going in life. We must replace this negative fuel with positive fuel, which will come from creating feel-good dopamine associations within our subconscious mind.

Thankfully there is hope to creating feel-good dopamine associations in our everyday life, and where there's hope, there's a way. We can talk directly to our subconscious mind through affirmations and have a reversing effect from the negative build-up of cortisol we've acquired through fears, doubts, and uncertainty.

YOUR WORDS ARE VERY POWERFUL! A lot of what you do and the actions that follow that affect you are a product of your words, whether intentionally or unintentionally said. The unintentional words are both the most important and the most dangerous because they come from your subconscious mind. The moment we speak out loud, the words that are said become an energy magnet for what was just said. Spitting out doubts about your circumstance will bring just that—doubt and worry. This can also leads to a build-up of cortisol in your body and a lack of confidence in accomplishing what you want. Instead, speak only what you want to happen and what you believe is happening for you right now. In the next section I am going to explain how we can actively speak directly to our subconscious mind, so we can begin a new journey to our goals with happiness and freedom.

R&R
RECOGNITION & REJECTION

All you need is some R&R in your life—recognition and rejection. You can't reject negative self-sabotaging thoughts and doubts unless you recognize when you are having them. Let me say that again for the people in the back… THE ONLY WAY TO REJECT IS TO RECOGNIZE. Our brains are our greatest muscles, so we must build them up to work in our favor. Saying positive affirmations out loud will create positive and forward-thinking energy within our minds, building our brain muscles to fight resistance towards our fears, and with this built-up resistance we can recognize when a negative thought comes into our minds. In order to recognize the negative thought, you need to train your mind to think positively a majority of the time so that when a negative thought does come, you can identify that thought to be not true from the positive thoughts you have built up, and reject it.

You will be able to feel it. There will be a substantial change in the energy shift that you will feel from positive to negative in your body that will be a prime indicator of something being off within your mind. This feeling will most likely come from your solar plexus—the area around the top of your stomach where you feel butterflies when you are excited or queasy if you have anxiety. So if you are ever feeling uneasy about a goal of yours, the solar plexus will be a telltale sign of how you may be thinking toward the situation, and recognizing this will allow you to reject any negative notion. We are inundated with social media daily by people who either seem like they have life figured out or by people that pressure you to figure yours out, and this can create a cocktail of emotions that can make life feel difficult. It is important to listen to your own thoughts towards your goals and verbally reassure yourself that you can be who you desire to be.

    Knowing about yourself and who you are is the most important investment you can make in this life. I am not just talking about your physical self, but your mental self. Thoughts are very powerful, and what you think about is what you will become. What you thought about has dictated who you are now. Changing your thoughts allows you to change who you are going to be. This is powerful because you must realize you can actively change who you are for the better, and not the other way around, if you think carefully. Recognizing a negative thought and why you are having that thought, can allow to you to correct yourself to think positively and attack the circumstance that made you have that negative thought in the first place.

    Answers for us are in our minds. Everything in this world has been created from a thought. How are things in this world created? For every physical creation someone had to think. The great Bob Proctor once said that every invention in this world was created from a collection of thoughts. We pull thoughts into our minds, and we build pictures or images to visualize a physical creation. A lot of these physical creations have become essential in our everyday life, all of which have occurred from a thought. You can use this same technique on yourself. Once you build an image of something in your mind, you are capable of building a physical replica of it in your world. So if you build an image of yourself as a joyous and calm person or a happy and confident person, you can live like that. If you can build an image of abundance and prosperity, you can live abundantly and prosperously.

What you think you desire in life is what you can have, and it is very important that you are specific. Never think to yourself that you can't have what you want. Eliminate these negative thoughts by recognizing and rejecting these negative thoughts. Once you train your mind to think positively by using positive affirmations, it will be easy to recognize the negative thought once it hits your mind. The gravitational pull of what you want will start to happen once you start collecting positive thoughts toward what you want.

Would you ever try to stop a freight train going 80 miles per hour dead in its tracks? If you're like most sane people, then the answer is HELL NO! Your mind can be an unstoppable train of positive thoughts leading you to your goals. The universe will not get in your way once you put together in your mind positive thought after positive thought, creating a freight train of positive thoughts leading you to your destination. Once you build that positive train of momentum, any negative thoughts of doubt on that track to your destiny will be demolished. The negative thoughts will be easier to identify once you are accustomed to thinking positively. If you don't already think positively a majority of the time then the opposite may be true right now. If this is the case—as is the case with 80 percent of humans according to a research conducted by the National Science Foundation—then recognize your brain is set up this way, begin saying positive affirmations out loud to reject these thoughts, and start the process of reversing how you think a majority of the time.

If you don't agree with an idea that pops into your head, then reject the idea. If that idea goes against what you believe yourself to be and what you believe yourself to become, then reject the idea. Once you identify where you are going in your mind, you paint the picture of your destination and lay the groundwork to make that destination real.

The people who you hang around with can influence your way of thinking as well. You know that old adage "you are who you hang out with," that you hear from time to time? Well that is true. Just as I say "you are who you think you are," that applies to who's thinking out loud around you as well. You can think positive all you want and have built up that train of positive thoughts, but if the train of negative thoughts in your circle is a greater force against your train of positive thoughts, it can be a difficult road to reach your goals. Now, the next time you are around the people in your circle, recognize the language being used around you, and if it is not positive language catering to you, you must reject the language being used. You can do this in two ways. The first way would be to simply leave the conversation and focus on the positive thoughts that you want to think. The other way, which can create a more powerful force in your favor, is to interrupt whoever is speaking the negative language and reinforce positive language about the situation they are discussing. If they are able to change their way of thinking in a positive way, this can create an even more powerful and positive force of energy within your circle that allows you to achieve your goals even faster. If they aren't able to change their way of thinking, you have the power to choose whether to stay in the conversation and trust your positive thoughts are more powerful than the negative thoughts that are being spoken, or you can just exit the conversation. Ultimately you have the power to choose.

We can be our own worst enemies at times. Just as we are thinking of something that may revolutionize our lives or be a major accomplishment for us, we can sometimes immediately psych ourselves out of the possibility of the outcome by overthinking and asking ourselves *how*, instead of just proceeding to follow that thought up with action. Telling yourself out loud that you can achieve that goal and reassuring yourself that you are successful in your journey to get there, can give you the confidence to achieve those goals because you will truly start to believe what you are saying the more you repeat it.

HOW TO USE AFFIRMATIONS

There are several different ways of using affirmations, but to get the most out your affirmations you want to make sure that you ground yourself, and get into what I like to call the "Ultra-Awareness" state. Within this state you are present with yourself, with where you are, and with how you are feeling in that moment. You can get into the Ultra-Awareness state in five simple steps.

First, you want to make sure that you are in a position to be comfortable and be still. You can find yourself in this position when you first wake up in your bed, on the floor of your bedroom or living room, sitting on the couch, or anywhere that you are comfortable and can be still. Whatever you do, make sure that your body is in an upright position.

Second, you are going to put your phone away and silence and turn off any electronic devices around you. One notification *ding* from an app on your phone can take you out of the Ultra-Awareness state in an instant. You may consciously not mind that notification ding, but we are catering to your delicate subconscious mind. No need to have your subconscious mind worry about who or what that *ding* notification was about, effectively detouring you from the journey to get to where you want to be.

Third, you are going to close your eyes and breathe deeply, focusing on the pace of your breaths. Take 3 seconds to breathe in through your nose, and then take 7 seconds to breathe out through your mouth. After a few breaths, you should notice a rhythm with the sound of your breathing similar to the sound of waves washing on the beach.

Fourth, while you are doing this breathing technique, notice how you are feeling in your current state, both physically and emotionally. Physically, notice any aches or pains, if any at all, you may be experiencing in this state. For example, if you are in a position where your legs are folded while sitting down, you may notice a stretch in your hips or quads. Emotionally, notice how you are feeling in this state, whether that feeling is happiness, sadness, confusion, doubt, or nothing at all, which is perfectly fine and a normal feeling in itself. Whatever you are feeling emotionally in this state, it is critical you acknowledge it. Connecting your physical state to your mental state gets you halfway to the Ultra-Awareness state.

You will ultimately get to the Ultra-Awareness state by completing the fifth and final step. So on this fifth step, once you have acknowledged how you are feeling physically and emotionally, think back to a time when you were happy and enjoying yourself. This moment in time could have been a split second, a few days, or somewhere in between. Now really think about this moment. Was it a trip or vacation somewhere? Was it a time you were laughing about a certain joke or experience with your family member or friend? Was it a certain food you ate for the first time? Was it how a certain somebody made you feel in a moment? Whichever moment resonates with you, take that moment, while maintaining your breathing technique, and LIVE in it. You may notice yourself smiling because you truly feel like you are now back in that moment that made you happy. When you are LIVING in that moment, while maintaining your breathing technique, being cognizant of your physical and mental state, and then realizing that you have successfully changed your mood from your previous state to your LIVING state, you have then reached the Ultra-Awareness state. While you are in this state, start saying your affirmations out loud.

Whatever you desire, you need to make them real and visually tangible. In the Ultra-Awareness state, you have reached a very powerful frame of mind, one where your energy vibrations are up and the gravitational pull of your desires become stronger to you because you are now able to harness and control how you choose to feel. Please do not waste the power of this moment. Say your positive affirmations out loud in this moment, and don't be embarrassed. Yes, it may feel awkward at first, but this feeling will subside as you start repeating and believing the affirmations you are saying out loud. Saying positive affirmations out loud can not only motivate you, but it can take everything you want from the mental realm and put them into the physical realm. Saying affirmations out loud makes them real. Seeing yourself in the position to receive the affirmation you are saying out loud makes your desire visually tangible. This is your greatest strength, and you must realize that it came from within you. Realize that you are in control of making your desires come true. It is important to note that consistency is key, and over time while saying your affirmations out loud and practicing the Ultra-Awareness technique, your mind will change for the better.

The Ultra-Awareness state allows you to be in control of your inner self and your external surroundings. Once you can identify how you are feeling and control how you really *want* to feel, you will be more aware of the energies around you. You will be able to have the ability to decide if you can control the energies around you to cater towards how you want to feel, or have the power within you to distance yourself from the negative energy that you can't control.

    To overcome self-sabotaging, negative, and doubting thoughts you must speak to your subconscious mind. Your subconscious thoughts are just as important—if not more important—than your conscious thoughts. While you are on this life journey with your body being the vehicle and your conscious mind being the engine or motor that keeps you going, your subconscious mind is what drives you on autopilot without conscious thought. Have you every been driving to a destination, in the process you're listening to music, thinking about what you are going to eat, what your plans are for that day, or what someone said to you, and then, in what seems like a blink of an eye, you are at your destination? Or have you ever zoned out mid-conversation with someone because you were thinking about something else that you had to do, but then that someone asked you a question and you were then able to answer that question as if you were truly engaged in the conversation? Your conscious mind was in a million different places in each scenario, but your subconscious mind was on autopilot, keeping you safe on the road while switching lanes to your destination and keeping notes of what the other person was saying in conversation so you were able to articulate an answer as if you never left. Your subconscious mind was trained over time in these scenarios to act accordingly, and you must do the same when it comes to changing negative thoughts into positive thoughts. Using positive words of affirmation out loud will make your subconscious mind believe them and over time flush out negative, debilitating thoughts that make it damn near impossible for you to see a path to your true desires. You can change your mind for the better. NEVER say that you can't! Remember—words are powerful, and you must use them in your favor.

♦ THE ULTRA-AWARENESS STATE ♦

1. Find a comfortable position and be still.

2. Put your phone away and turn off all electronic devices.

3. Close your eyes. Take deep breaths, focusing on the pace: 3 seconds in through your nose and 7 seconds out through your mouth.

4. Notice your current physical and emotional state.

5. Remember a happy moment in your life, and live in it.

FULFILLMENT JOURNAL PURPOSE

Combining writing with saying your positive affirmations out loud is powerful. Taking thoughts from your mind and putting them on paper makes them real. This makes what you want tangible. The daily fulfillment journal's purpose is to guide you to what you choose your life's destination to be. By answering the three questions in the journal and saying an affirmation to own your truth, you will effectively get to your destination. Be sure to say the affirmation that you write out loud and believe it, because that is your truth.

YOUR JOURNEY STARTS NOW

Being consistent is key. Every day that you move forward is another day closer to where you want to be. You are closer to the end of your journey than you are to the beginning, so don't look back. Go forward. Progression is on the other side of uncertainty. By reading this, you have already made the decision to progress your life and move forward without fear because you believe you deserve to live in your truth. Change your perception to change your reality. You are the shit, and don't your forget it!

AFFIRMATION

I AM
The Shit!

Repeat out loud 20 times.

(For best results look at yourself in the mirror
while repeating this statement.)

DAILY FULFILMENT JOURNAL

Date _/_/_

I AM grateful for…

_____
_____
_____

WHAT do I want?

_____
_____
_____

WHAT can I do today?

_____
_____
_____

Affirmation of the day: I AM, I CAN, I WILL, etc.

_____
_____
_____

AFFIRMATION

I AM attracting what I deserve.

Repeat out loud 20 times

(For best results look at yourself in the mirror while repeating this statement.)

DAILY FULFILMENT JOURNAL

Date _/_/_

I AM grateful for…

_____
_____
_____

WHAT do I want?

_____
_____
_____

WHAT can I do today?

_____
_____
_____

Affirmation of the day: I AM, I CAN, I WILL, etc.

_____
_____
_____

AFFIRMATION

I HAVE everything I need to be happy.

Repeat out loud 20 times

(For best results look at yourself in the mirror while repeating this statement.)

DAILY FULFILMENT JOURNAL

Date _/_/_

I AM grateful for…

_____
_____
_____

WHAT do I want?

_____
_____
_____

WHAT can I do today?

_____
_____
_____

Affirmation of the day: I AM, I CAN, I WILL, etc.

_____
_____
_____

AFFIRMATION

I LOVE myself completely.

Repeat out loud 20 times

(For best results look at yourself in the mirror while repeating this statement.)

DAILY FULFILMENT JOURNAL

Date _/_/_

I AM grateful for…

___

WHAT do I want?

___

WHAT can I do today?

___

Affirmation of the day: I AM, I CAN, I WILL, etc.

___

AFFIRMATION

I AM succeeding in my life.

Repeat out loud 20 times

(For best results look at yourself in the mirror while repeating this statement.)

DAILY FULFILMENT JOURNAL

Date _/_/_

I AM grateful for…

_____
_____
_____

WHAT do I want?

_____
_____
_____

WHAT can I do today?

_____
_____
_____

Affirmation of the day: I AM, I CAN, I WILL, etc.

_____
_____
_____

AFFIRMATION

I WILL NOT lose today.

Repeat out loud 20 times

(For best results look at yourself in the mirror while repeating this statement.)

DAILY FULFILMENT JOURNAL

Date _/_/_

I AM grateful for…

_____
_____
_____

WHAT do I want?

_____
_____
_____

WHAT can I do today?

_____
_____
_____

Affirmation of the day: I AM, I CAN, I WILL, etc.

_____
_____
_____

AFFIRMATION

I AM CONFIDENT in my abilities and myself.

Repeat out loud 20 times

(For best results look at yourself in the mirror while repeating this statement.)

DAILY FULFILMENT JOURNAL

Date _/_/_

I AM grateful for...

_____
_____
_____

WHAT do I want?

_____
_____
_____

WHAT can I do today?

_____
_____
_____

Affirmation of the day: I AM, I CAN, I WILL, etc.

_____
_____
_____

AFFIRMATION

I AM right where I am supposed to be.

Repeat out loud 20 times

(For best results look at yourself in the mirror while repeating this statement.)

DAILY FULFILMENT JOURNAL

Date _/_/_

I AM grateful for…

_____
_____
_____

WHAT do I want?

_____
_____
_____

WHAT can I do today?

_____
_____
_____

Affirmation of the day: I AM, I CAN, I WILL, etc.

_____
_____
_____

AFFIRMATION

I AM present to receive positive blessings.

Repeat out loud 20 times

(For best results look at yourself in the mirror while repeating this statement.)

DAILY FULFILMENT JOURNAL

Date _/_/_

I AM grateful for…

_____
_____
_____

WHAT do I want?

_____
_____
_____

WHAT can I do today?

_____
_____
_____

Affirmation of the day: I AM, I CAN, I WILL, etc.

_____
_____
_____

AFFIRMATION

I AM in command of my life.

Repeat out loud 20 times

(For best results look at yourself in the mirror while repeating this statement.)

DAILY FULFILMENT JOURNAL

Date _/_/_

I AM grateful for…

_____
_____
_____

WHAT do I want?

_____
_____
_____

WHAT can I do today?

_____
_____
_____

Affirmation of the day: I AM, I CAN, I WILL, etc.

_____
_____
_____

AFFIRMATION

I AM valuable.

Repeat out loud 20 times

(For best results look at yourself in the mirror while repeating this statement.)

DAILY FULFILMENT JOURNAL

Date _/_/_

I AM grateful for...
_____
_____
_____

WHAT do I want?
_____
_____
_____

WHAT can I do today?
_____
_____
_____

Affirmation of the day: I AM, I CAN, I WILL, etc.
_____
_____
_____

AFFIRMATION

I AM the director of my movie.

Repeat out loud 20 times

(For best results look at yourself in the mirror while repeating this statement.)

DAILY FULFILMENT JOURNAL

Date _/_/_

I AM grateful for…

_____
_____
_____

WHAT do I want?

_____
_____
_____

WHAT can I do today?

_____
_____
_____

Affirmation of the day: I AM, I CAN, I WILL, etc.

_____
_____
_____

AFFIRMATION

I HAVE an abundance of opportunities in front of me.

Repeat out loud 20 times

(For best results look at yourself in the mirror while repeating this statement.)

DAILY FULFILMENT JOURNAL

Date _/_/_

I AM grateful for…

_____
_____
_____

WHAT do I want?

_____
_____
_____

WHAT can I do today?

_____
_____
_____

Affirmation of the day: I AM, I CAN, I WILL, etc.

_____
_____
_____

AFFIRMATION

I AM in control of my surroundings.

Repeat out loud 20 times

(For best results look at yourself in the mirror while repeating this statement.)

DAILY FULFILMENT JOURNAL

Date _/_/_

I AM grateful for...

_____
_____
_____

WHAT do I want?

_____
_____
_____

WHAT can I do today?

_____
_____
_____

Affirmation of the day: I AM, I CAN, I WILL, etc.

_____
_____
_____

AFFIRMATION

I RELEASE all doubt from my mind.

Repeat out loud 20 times

(For best results look at yourself in the mirror while repeating this statement.)

DAILY FULFILMENT JOURNAL

Date _/_/_

I AM grateful for…

_____
_____
_____

WHAT do I want?

_____
_____
_____

WHAT can I do today?

_____
_____
_____

Affirmation of the day: I AM, I CAN, I WILL, etc.

_____
_____
_____

AFFIRMATION

I CAN do this today.

Repeat out loud 20 times

(For best results look at yourself in the mirror while repeating this statement.)

DAILY FULFILMENT JOURNAL

Date _/_/_

I AM grateful for…
_____
_____
_____

WHAT do I want?
_____
_____
_____

WHAT can I do today?
_____
_____
_____

Affirmation of the day: I AM, I CAN, I WILL, etc.
_____
_____
_____

AFFIRMATION

I AM
enough.

Repeat out loud 20 times

(For best results look at yourself in the mirror while repeating this statement.)

DAILY FULFILMENT JOURNAL

Date _/_/_

I AM grateful for…

_____
_____
_____

WHAT do I want?

_____
_____
_____

WHAT can I do today?

_____
_____
_____

Affirmation of the day: I AM, I CAN, I WILL, etc.

_____
_____
_____

AFFIRMATION

I AM not done and my life is just beginning.

Repeat out loud 20 times

(For best results look at yourself in the mirror while repeating this statement.)

DAILY FULFILMENT JOURNAL

Date _/_/_

I AM grateful for…

_____
_____
_____

WHAT do I want?

_____
_____
_____

WHAT can I do today?

_____
_____
_____

Affirmation of the day: I AM, I CAN, I WILL, etc.

_____
_____
_____

AFFIRMATION

I RELEASE all negative energy from around me.

Repeat out loud 20 times

(For best results look at yourself in the mirror while repeating this statement.)

DAILY FULFILMENT JOURNAL

Date _/_/_

I AM grateful for…

_____
_____
_____

WHAT do I want?

_____
_____

WHAT can I do today?

_____
_____

Affirmation of the day: I AM, I CAN, I WILL, etc.

_____
_____

AFFIRMATION

I AM attracting positive energy.

Repeat out loud 20 times

(For best results look at yourself in the mirror while repeating this statement.)

DAILY FULFILMENT JOURNAL

Date _/_/_

I AM grateful for…

_____
_____
_____

WHAT do I want?

_____
_____
_____

WHAT can I do today?

_____
_____
_____

Affirmation of the day: I AM, I CAN, I WILL, etc.

_____
_____
_____

AFFIRMATION

I AM a positive person.

Repeat out loud 20 times

(For best results look at yourself in the mirror while repeating this statement.)

DAILY FULFILMENT JOURNAL

Date _/_/_

I AM grateful for…

_____
_____
_____

WHAT do I want?

_____
_____
_____

WHAT can I do today?

_____
_____
_____

Affirmation of the day: I AM, I CAN, I WILL, etc.

_____
_____
_____

AFFIRMATION

I WILL stay positive in the face of adversity.

Repeat out loud 20 times

(For best results look at yourself in the mirror while repeating this statement.)

DAILY FULFILMENT JOURNAL

Date _/_/_

I AM grateful for…

___
___
___

WHAT do I want?

___
___

WHAT can I do today?

___
___

Affirmation of the day: I AM, I CAN, I WILL, etc.

___
___

AFFIRMATION

I WILL NOT overreact to things I can not change.

Repeat out loud 20 times

(For best results look at yourself in the mirror while repeating this statement.)

DAILY FULFILMENT JOURNAL

Date _/_/_

I AM grateful for…
_____
_____
_____

WHAT do I want?
_____
_____
_____

WHAT can I do today?
_____
_____
_____

Affirmation of the day: I AM, I CAN, I WILL, etc.
_____
_____
_____

AFFIRMATION

I AM
happy.

Repeat out loud 20 times

(For best results look at yourself in the mirror while repeating this statement **AND SMILE!**)

DAILY FULFILMENT JOURNAL

Date _/_/_

I AM grateful for…

_____
_____
_____

WHAT do I want?

_____
_____
_____

WHAT can I do today?

_____
_____
_____

Affirmation of the day: I AM, I CAN, I WILL, etc.

_____
_____
_____

AFFIRMATION

I AM winning today.

Repeat out loud 20 times

(For best results look at yourself in the mirror while repeating this statement.)

DAILY FULFILMENT JOURNAL

Date _/_/_

I AM grateful for…

_____
_____
_____

WHAT do I want?

_____
_____
_____

WHAT can I do today?

_____
_____
_____

Affirmation of the day: I AM, I CAN, I WILL, etc.

_____
_____
_____

AFFIRMATION

I AM closer to my dreams today.

Repeat out loud 20 times

(For best results look at yourself in the mirror while repeating this statement.)

DAILY FULFILMENT JOURNAL

Date _/_/_

I AM grateful for…

_____
_____
_____

WHAT do I want?

_____
_____
_____

WHAT can I do today?

_____
_____
_____

Affirmation of the day: I AM, I CAN, I WILL, etc.

_____
_____
_____

AFFIRMATION

I RELEASE all self-sabotaging thoughts.

Repeat out loud 20 times

(For best results look at yourself in the mirror while repeating this statement.)

DAILY FULFILMENT JOURNAL

Date _/_/_

I AM grateful for…

_____
_____
_____

WHAT do I want?

_____
_____
_____

WHAT can I do today?

_____
_____
_____

Affirmation of the day: I AM, I CAN, I WILL, etc.

_____
_____

AFFIRMATION

I AM sure of my decisions.

Repeat out loud 20 times

(For best results look at yourself in the mirror while repeating this statement.)

DAILY FULFILMENT JOURNAL

Date _/_/_

I AM grateful for…

_____
_____
_____

WHAT do I want?

_____
_____
_____

WHAT can I do today?

_____
_____
_____

Affirmation of the day: I AM, I CAN, I WILL, etc.

_____
_____
_____

AFFIRMATION

I FEEL attractive.

Repeat out loud 20 times

(For best results look at yourself in the mirror while repeating this statement.)

DAILY FULFILMENT JOURNAL

Date _/_/_

I AM grateful for…

_____
_____
_____

WHAT do I want?

_____
_____
_____

WHAT can I do today?

_____
_____
_____

Affirmation of the day: I AM, I CAN, I WILL, etc.

_____
_____
_____

AFFIRMATION

I HAVE a beautiful soul.

Repeat out loud 20 times

(For best results look at yourself in the mirror while repeating this statement.)

DAILY FULFILMENT JOURNAL

Date _/_/_

I AM grateful for…

_____
_____
_____

WHAT do I want?

_____
_____
_____

WHAT can I do today?

_____
_____
_____

Affirmation of the day: I AM, I CAN, I WILL, etc.

_____
_____
_____

AFFIRMATION

I AM worthy of love.

Repeat out loud 20 times

(For best results look at yourself in the mirror while repeating this statement.)

DAILY FULFILMENT JOURNAL

Date _/_/_

I AM grateful for…
_____
_____
_____

WHAT do I want?
_____
_____

WHAT can I do today?
_____
_____
_____

Affirmation of the day: I AM, I CAN, I WILL, etc.
_____
_____
_____

AFFIRMATION

I AM
charismatic.

Repeat out loud 20 times

(For best results look at yourself in the mirror
while repeating this statement.)

DAILY FULFILMENT JOURNAL

Date _/_/_

I AM grateful for...
_____
_____
_____

WHAT do I want?
_____
_____

WHAT can I do today?
_____
_____

Affirmation of the day: I AM, I CAN, I WILL, etc.
_____
_____

AFFIRMATION

I ONLY see solutions, not problems.

Repeat out loud 20 times

(For best results look at yourself in the mirror while repeating this statement.)

DAILY FULFILMENT JOURNAL

Date _/_/_

I AM grateful for...
_____
_____
_____

WHAT do I want?
_____
_____
_____

WHAT can I do today?
_____
_____
_____

Affirmation of the day: I AM, I CAN, I WILL, etc.
_____
_____

AFFIRMATION

I WILL be clear and direct with my intentions.

Repeat out loud 20 times

(For best results look at yourself in the mirror while repeating this statement.)

DAILY FULFILMENT JOURNAL

Date _/_/_

I AM grateful for…

_____
_____
_____

WHAT do I want?

_____
_____
_____

WHAT can I do today?

_____
_____
_____

Affirmation of the day: I AM, I CAN, I WILL, etc.

_____
_____
_____

AFFIRMATION

I AM responsible for my life.

Repeat out loud 20 times

(For best results look at yourself in the mirror while repeating this statement.)

DAILY FULFILMENT JOURNAL

Date _/_/_

I AM grateful for…

_____
_____
_____

WHAT do I want?

_____
_____
_____

WHAT can I do today?

_____
_____
_____

Affirmation of the day: I AM, I CAN, I WILL, etc.

_____
_____
_____

AFFIRMATION

I HAVE the power to change my habits.

Repeat out loud 20 times

(For best results look at yourself in the mirror while repeating this statement.)

DAILY FULFILMENT JOURNAL

Date _/_/_

I AM grateful for...

___

WHAT do I want?

___

WHAT can I do today?

___

Affirmation of the day: I AM, I CAN, I WILL, etc.

___

AFFIRMATION

TODAY I release my bad habits and replace them with new positive habits.

Repeat out loud 20 times

(For best results look at yourself in the mirror while repeating this statement.)

DAILY FULFILMENT JOURNAL

Date _/_/_

I AM grateful for…

_____
_____
_____

WHAT do I want?

_____
_____
_____

WHAT can I do today?

_____
_____
_____

Affirmation of the day: I AM, I CAN, I WILL, etc.

_____
_____
_____

AFFIRMATION

I AM worthy of the best things in life, and I accept them now.

Repeat out loud 20 times

(For best results look at yourself in the mirror while repeating this statement.)

DAILY FULFILMENT JOURNAL

Date _/_/_

I AM grateful for…

_____
_____
_____

WHAT do I want?

_____
_____
_____

WHAT can I do today?

_____
_____
_____

Affirmation of the day: I AM, I CAN, I WILL, etc.

_____
_____
_____

AFFIRMATION

I RELEASE the negative things that I can not change.

Repeat out loud 20 times

(For best results look at yourself in the mirror while repeating this statement.)

DAILY FULFILMENT JOURNAL

Date _/_/_

I AM grateful for…

_____
_____
_____

WHAT do I want?

_____
_____
_____

WHAT can I do today?

_____
_____
_____

Affirmation of the day: I AM, I CAN, I WILL, etc.

_____
_____
_____

AFFIRMATION

I WILL NOT dwell on my past.

Repeat out loud 20 times

(For best results look at yourself in the mirror while repeating this statement.)

DAILY FULFILMENT JOURNAL

Date _/_/_

I AM grateful for…
_____
_____
_____

WHAT do I want?
_____
_____
_____

WHAT can I do today?
_____
_____
_____

Affirmation of the day: I AM, I CAN, I WILL, etc.
_____
_____
_____

AFFIRMATION

I FEEL good and healthy.

Repeat out loud 20 times

(For best results look at yourself in the mirror while repeating this statement.)

DAILY FULFILMENT JOURNAL

Date _/_/_

I AM grateful for…

_____
_____
_____

WHAT do I want?

_____
_____
_____

WHAT can I do today?

_____
_____
_____

Affirmation of the day: I AM, I CAN, I WILL, etc.

_____
_____
_____

AFFIRMATION

I HAVE a healthy immune system.

Repeat out loud 20 times

(For best results look at yourself in the mirror while repeating this statement.)

DAILY FULFILMENT JOURNAL

Date _/_/_

I AM grateful for…

_____
_____
_____

WHAT do I want?

_____
_____
_____

WHAT can I do today?

_____
_____
_____

Affirmation of the day: I AM, I CAN, I WILL, etc.

_____
_____
_____

AFFIRMATION

I KNOW I am making progress daily.

Repeat out loud 20 times

(For best results look at yourself in the mirror while repeating this statement.)

DAILY FULFILMENT JOURNAL

Date _/_/_

I AM grateful for…

_____
_____
_____

WHAT do I want?

_____
_____

WHAT can I do today?

_____
_____

Affirmation of the day: I AM, I CAN, I WILL, etc.

_____
_____
_____

AFFIRMATION

NOTHING and NO ONE can hold me back.

Repeat out loud 20 times

(For best results look at yourself in the mirror while repeating this statement.)

DAILY FULFILMENT JOURNAL

Date _/_/_

I AM grateful for…

_____
_____
_____

WHAT do I want?

_____
_____
_____

WHAT can I do today?

_____
_____
_____

Affirmation of the day: I AM, I CAN, I WILL, etc.

_____
_____
_____

AFFIRMATION

I AM an unstoppable force.

Repeat out loud 20 times

(For best results look at yourself in the mirror while repeating this statement.)

DAILY FULFILMENT JOURNAL

Date _/_/_

I AM grateful for...

_____
_____
_____

WHAT do I want?

_____
_____
_____

WHAT can I do today?

_____
_____
_____

Affirmation of the day: I AM, I CAN, I WILL, etc.

_____
_____
_____

AFFIRMATION

NOTHING and NO ONE can steal my joy.

Repeat out loud 20 times

(For best results look at yourself in the mirror while repeating this statement.)

DAILY FULFILMENT JOURNAL

Date _/_/_

I AM grateful for…

_____
_____
_____

WHAT do I want?

_____
_____
_____

WHAT can I do today?

_____
_____
_____

Affirmation of the day: I AM, I CAN, I WILL, etc.

_____
_____
_____

AFFIRMATION

Everything's gon' be okay.

Repeat out loud 20 times

(For best results look at yourself in the mirror while repeating this statement.)

DAILY FULFILMENT JOURNAL

Date _/_/_

I AM grateful for…

_____
_____
_____

WHAT do I want?

_____
_____
_____

WHAT can I do today?

_____
_____
_____

Affirmation of the day: I AM, I CAN, I WILL, etc.

_____
_____
_____

AFFIRMATION

I HAVE been divinely ordered to be great.

Repeat out loud 20 times

(For best results look at yourself in the mirror while repeating this statement.)

DAILY FULFILMENT JOURNAL

Date _/_/_

I AM grateful for...
_____
_____
_____

WHAT do I want?
_____
_____
_____

WHAT can I do today?
_____
_____
_____

Affirmation of the day: I AM, I CAN, I WILL, etc.
_____
_____
_____

AFFIRMATION

I ACCEPT me for who I am.

Repeat out loud 20 times

(For best results look at yourself in the mirror while repeating this statement.)

DAILY FULFILMENT JOURNAL

Date _/_/_

I AM grateful for…

_____
_____
_____

WHAT do I want?

_____
_____
_____

WHAT can I do today?

_____
_____
_____

Affirmation of the day: I AM, I CAN, I WILL, etc.

_____
_____
_____

AFFIRMATION

I RELEASE any resentment I have ever had.

Repeat out loud 20 times

(For best results look at yourself in the mirror while repeating this statement.)

DAILY FULFILMENT JOURNAL

Date _/_/_

I AM grateful for…

_____
_____
_____

WHAT do I want?

_____
_____
_____

WHAT can I do today?

_____
_____
_____

Affirmation of the day: I AM, I CAN, I WILL, etc.

_____
_____
_____

AFFIRMATION

I RELEASE all sadness from my body.

Repeat out loud 20 times

(For best results look at yourself in the mirror while repeating this statement.)

DAILY FULFILMENT JOURNAL

Date _/_/_

I AM grateful for…

_____
_____
_____

WHAT do I want?

_____
_____
_____

WHAT can I do today?

_____
_____
_____

Affirmation of the day: I AM, I CAN, I WILL, etc.

_____
_____
_____

AFFIRMATION

I CHOOSE to be my best self while I am alone.

Repeat out loud 20 times

(For best results look at yourself in the mirror while repeating this statement.)

DAILY FULFILMENT JOURNAL

Date _/_/_

I AM grateful for…

_____
_____
_____

WHAT do I want?

_____
_____
_____

WHAT can I do today?

_____
_____
_____

Affirmation of the day: I AM, I CAN, I WILL, etc.

_____
_____
_____

AFFIRMATION

I AM resilient.

Repeat out loud 20 times

(For best results look at yourself in the mirror while repeating this statement.)

DAILY FULFILMENT JOURNAL

Date _/_/_

I AM grateful for...

_____
_____
_____

WHAT do I want?

_____
_____
_____

WHAT can I do today?

_____
_____
_____

Affirmation of the day: I AM, I CAN, I WILL, etc.

_____
_____
_____

AFFIRMATION

I KNOW money will come to me in easy, consistent, and unexpected ways.

Repeat out loud 20 times

(For best results look at yourself in the mirror while repeating this statement.)

DAILY FULFILMENT JOURNAL

Date _/_/_

I AM grateful for…

_____
_____
_____

WHAT do I want?

_____
_____
_____

WHAT can I do today?

_____
_____
_____

Affirmation of the day: I AM, I CAN, I WILL, etc.

_____
_____
_____

AFFIRMATION

I WILL NOT let money define my happiness.

Repeat out loud 20 times

(For best results look at yourself in the mirror while repeating this statement.)

DAILY FULFILMENT JOURNAL

Date _/_/_

I AM grateful for…

_____
_____
_____

WHAT do I want?

_____
_____
_____

WHAT can I do today?

_____
_____
_____

Affirmation of the day: I AM, I CAN, I WILL, etc.

_____
_____
_____

AFFIRMATION

MY mind is in tune with my body.

Repeat out loud 20 times

(For best results look at yourself in the mirror while repeating this statement.)

DAILY FULFILMENT JOURNAL

Date _/_/_

I AM grateful for…
_____
_____
_____

WHAT do I want?
_____
_____
_____

WHAT can I do today?
_____
_____
_____

Affirmation of the day: I AM, I CAN, I WILL, etc.
_____
_____

AFFIRMATION

I AM strong.

Repeat out loud 20 times

(For best results look at yourself in the mirror while repeating this statement.)

DAILY FULFILMENT JOURNAL

Date _/_/_

I AM grateful for…

_____
_____
_____

WHAT do I want?

_____
_____
_____

WHAT can I do today?

_____
_____
_____

Affirmation of the day: I AM, I CAN, I WILL, etc.

_____
_____
_____

AFFIRMATION

I CHOOSE to rely on my own judgment.

Repeat out loud 20 times

(For best results look at yourself in the mirror while repeating this statement.)

DAILY FULFILMENT JOURNAL

Date _/_/_

I AM grateful for…
_____
_____
_____

WHAT do I want?
_____
_____

WHAT can I do today?
_____
_____

Affirmation of the day: I AM, I CAN, I WILL, etc.
_____
_____
_____

AFFIRMATION

I TRUST my intuition.

Repeat out loud 20 times

(For best results look at yourself in the mirror while repeating this statement.)

DAILY FULFILMENT JOURNAL

Date _/_/_

I AM grateful for...

_____
_____
_____

WHAT do I want?

_____
_____
_____

WHAT can I do today?

_____
_____
_____

Affirmation of the day: I AM, I CAN, I WILL, etc.

_____
_____
_____

AFFIRMATION

I WILL NOT let fear exist in my life.

Repeat out loud 20 times

(For best results look at yourself in the mirror while repeating this statement.)

DAILY FULFILMENT JOURNAL

Date _/_/_

I AM grateful for…

_____
_____
_____

WHAT do I want?

_____
_____
_____

WHAT can I do today?

_____
_____
_____

Affirmation of the day: I AM, I CAN, I WILL, etc.

_____
_____
_____

AFFIRMATION

MY existence in this world will make an impact.

Repeat out loud 20 times

(For best results look at yourself in the mirror while repeating this statement.)

DAILY FULFILMENT JOURNAL

Date _/_/_

I AM grateful for…

_____
_____
_____

WHAT do I want?

_____
_____
_____

WHAT can I do today?

_____
_____
_____

Affirmation of the day: I AM, I CAN, I WILL, etc.

_____
_____
_____

AFFIRMATION

I WILL not believe the lie that "I can't."

Repeat out loud 20 times

(For best results look at yourself in the mirror while repeating this statement.)

DAILY FULFILMENT JOURNAL

Date _/_/_

I AM grateful for...

_____
_____
_____

WHAT do I want?

_____
_____
_____

WHAT can I do today?

_____
_____
_____

Affirmation of the day: I AM, I CAN, I WILL, etc.

_____
_____
_____

AFFIRMATION

I HAVE no doubts about my future.

Repeat out loud 20 times

(For best results look at yourself in the mirror while repeating this statement.)

DAILY FULFILMENT JOURNAL

Date _/_/_

I AM grateful for…

_____
_____
_____

WHAT do I want?

_____
_____
_____

WHAT can I do today?

_____
_____
_____

Affirmation of the day: I AM, I CAN, I WILL, etc.

_____
_____
_____

AFFIRMATION

MY authentic self will attract success.

Repeat out loud 20 times

(For best results look at yourself in the mirror while repeating this statement.)

DAILY FULFILMENT JOURNAL

Date _/_/_

I AM grateful for…

_____
_____
_____

WHAT do I want?

_____
_____

WHAT can I do today?

_____
_____

Affirmation of the day: I AM, I CAN, I WILL, etc.

_____
_____
_____

AFFIRMATION

MY journey is unique to me, and only I control my outcomes.

Repeat out loud 20 times

(For best results look at yourself in the mirror while repeating this statement.)

DAILY FULFILMENT JOURNAL

Date _/_/_

I AM grateful for…

_____
_____
_____

WHAT do I want?

_____
_____
_____

WHAT can I do today?

_____
_____
_____

Affirmation of the day: I AM, I CAN, I WILL, etc.

_____
_____
_____

AFFIRMATION

I CAN do anything that I believe in.

Repeat out loud 20 times

(For best results look at yourself in the mirror while repeating this statement.)

DAILY FULFILMENT JOURNAL

Date _/_/_

I AM grateful for…

_____
_____
_____

WHAT do I want?

_____
_____
_____

WHAT can I do today?

_____
_____
_____

Affirmation of the day: I AM, I CAN, I WILL, etc.

_____
_____
_____

AFFIRMATION

I AM a step closer to who I am destined to be.

Repeat out loud 20 times

(For best results look at yourself in the mirror while repeating this statement.)

DAILY FULFILMENT JOURNAL

Date _/_/_

I AM grateful for…

_____
_____
_____

WHAT do I want?

_____
_____
_____

WHAT can I do today?

_____
_____
_____

Affirmation of the day: I AM, I CAN, I WILL, etc.

_____
_____
_____

AFFIRMATION

MY destination in life is greater than what I can imagine.

Repeat out loud 20 times

(For best results look at yourself in the mirror while repeating this statement.)

DAILY FULFILMENT JOURNAL

Date _/_/_

I AM grateful for...

_____
_____
_____

WHAT do I want?

_____
_____
_____

WHAT can I do today?

_____
_____
_____

Affirmation of the day: I AM, I CAN, I WILL, etc.

_____
_____
_____

AFFIRMATION

I WILL achieve the goals I set for myself.

Repeat out loud 20 times

(For best results look at yourself in the mirror while repeating this statement.)

DAILY FULFILMENT JOURNAL

Date _/_/_

I AM grateful for...
_____
_____
_____

WHAT do I want?
_____
_____
_____

WHAT can I do today?
_____
_____
_____

Affirmation of the day: I AM, I CAN, I WILL, etc.
_____
_____
_____

AFFIRMATION

I AM God's masterpiece.

Repeat out loud 20 times

(For best results look at yourself in the mirror
while repeating this statement.)

DAILY FULFILMENT JOURNAL

Date _/_/_

I AM grateful for…
_____
_____
_____

WHAT do I want?
_____
_____

WHAT can I do today?
_____
_____

Affirmation of the day: I AM, I CAN, I WILL, etc.
_____
_____

AFFIRMATION

I WILL NOT be complacent.

Repeat out loud 20 times

(For best results look at yourself in the mirror
while repeating this statement.)

DAILY FULFILMENT JOURNAL

Date _/_/_

I AM grateful for…
_____
_____
_____

WHAT do I want?
_____
_____
_____

WHAT can I do today?
_____
_____
_____

Affirmation of the day: I AM, I CAN, I WILL, etc.
_____
_____
_____

AFFIRMATION

I WILL NOT let other people dictate my future.

Repeat out loud 20 times

(For best results look at yourself in the mirror while repeating this statement.)

DAILY FULFILMENT JOURNAL

Date _/_/_

I AM grateful for…

_____
_____
_____

WHAT do I want?

_____
_____
_____

WHAT can I do today?

_____
_____
_____

Affirmation of the day: I AM, I CAN, I WILL, etc.

_____
_____
_____

AFFIRMATION

I WILL NOT let other people control my talents.

Repeat out loud 20 times

(For best results look at yourself in the mirror while repeating this statement.)

DAILY FULFILMENT JOURNAL

Date _/_/_

I AM grateful for…

_____
_____
_____

WHAT do I want?

_____
_____
_____

WHAT can I do today?

_____
_____
_____

Affirmation of the day: I AM, I CAN, I WILL, etc.

_____
_____
_____

AFFIRMATION

I WILL NOT allow the actions of others to define how I view myself.

Repeat out loud 20 times

(For best results look at yourself in the mirror while repeating this statement.)

DAILY FULFILMENT JOURNAL

Date _/_/_

I AM grateful for…

_____
_____
_____

WHAT do I want?

_____
_____
_____

WHAT can I do today?

_____
_____
_____

Affirmation of the day: I AM, I CAN, I WILL, etc.

_____
_____
_____

AFFIRMATION

NO ONE can take away what is meant for me.

Repeat out loud 20 times

(For best results look at yourself in the mirror while repeating this statement.)

DAILY FULFILMENT JOURNAL

Date _/_/_

I AM grateful for...

_____
_____
_____

WHAT do I want?

_____
_____
_____

WHAT can I do today?

_____
_____
_____

Affirmation of the day: I AM, I CAN, I WILL, etc.

_____
_____
_____

AFFIRMATION

MY presence will be felt.

Repeat out loud 20 times

(For best results look at yourself in the mirror while repeating this statement.)

DAILY FULFILMENT JOURNAL

Date _/_/_

I AM grateful for...

_____
_____
_____

WHAT do I want?

_____
_____
_____

WHAT can I do today?

_____
_____
_____

Affirmation of the day: I AM, I CAN, I WILL, etc.

_____
_____
_____

AFFIRMATION

I AM focused on becoming my best self.

Repeat out loud 20 times

(For best results look at yourself in the mirror while repeating this statement.)

DAILY FULFILMENT JOURNAL

Date _/_/_

I AM grateful for…

_____
_____
_____

WHAT do I want?

_____
_____
_____

WHAT can I do today?

_____
_____
_____

Affirmation of the day: I AM, I CAN, I WILL, etc.

_____
_____
_____

AFFIRMATION

I AM motivated to go get what I desire.

Repeat out loud 20 times

(For best results look at yourself in the mirror while repeating this statement.)

DAILY FULFILMENT JOURNAL

Date _/_/_

I AM grateful for…

_____
_____
_____

WHAT do I want?

_____
_____
_____

WHAT can I do today?

_____
_____
_____

Affirmation of the day: I AM, I CAN, I WILL, etc.

_____
_____
_____

AFFIRMATION

I WILL do what I have to do today.

Repeat out loud 20 times

(For best results look at yourself in the mirror while repeating this statement.)

DAILY FULFILMENT JOURNAL

Date _/_/_

I AM grateful for…

_____
_____
_____

WHAT do I want?

_____
_____
_____

WHAT can I do today?

_____
_____
_____

Affirmation of the day: I AM, I CAN, I WILL, etc.

_____
_____
_____

AFFIRMATION

I AM different, and I am ok with that.

Repeat out loud 20 times

(For best results look at yourself in the mirror while repeating this statement.)

DAILY FULFILMENT JOURNAL

Date _/_/_

I AM grateful for...

_____
_____
_____

WHAT do I want?

_____
_____
_____

WHAT can I do today?

_____
_____
_____

Affirmation of the day: I AM, I CAN, I WILL, etc.

_____
_____
_____

AFFIRMATION

MY thoughts are what make me special.

Repeat out loud 20 times

(For best results look at yourself in the mirror while repeating this statement.)

DAILY FULFILMENT JOURNAL

Date _/_/_

I AM grateful for…

_____
_____
_____

WHAT do I want?

_____
_____
_____

WHAT can I do today?

_____
_____
_____

Affirmation of the day: I AM, I CAN, I WILL, etc.

_____
_____
_____

AFFIRMATION

I AM genuinely blessed.

Repeat out loud 20 times

(For best results look at yourself in the mirror while repeating this statement.)

DAILY FULFILMENT JOURNAL

Date _/_/_

I AM grateful for…
_____
_____
_____

WHAT do I want?
_____
_____
_____

WHAT can I do today?
_____
_____
_____

Affirmation of the day: I AM, I CAN, I WILL, etc.
_____
_____
_____

AFFIRMATION

I AM worth it.

Repeat out loud 20 times

(For best results look at yourself in the mirror while repeating this statement.)

DAILY FULFILMENT JOURNAL

Date _/_/_

I AM grateful for...
_____
_____
_____

WHAT do I want?
_____
_____
_____

WHAT can I do today?
_____
_____
_____

Affirmation of the day: I AM, I CAN, I WILL, etc.
_____
_____
_____

AFFIRMATION

I WILL receive my respect.

Repeat out loud 20 times

(For best results look at yourself in the mirror while repeating this statement.)

DAILY FULFILMENT JOURNAL

Date _/_/_

I AM grateful for…

_____
_____
_____

WHAT do I want?

_____
_____
_____

WHAT can I do today?

_____
_____
_____

Affirmation of the day: I AM, I CAN, I WILL, etc.

_____
_____
_____

AFFIRMATION

I AM
fearless.

Repeat out loud 20 times

(For best results look at yourself in the mirror
while repeating this statement.)

DAILY FULFILMENT JOURNAL

Date _/_/_

I AM grateful for…

_____
_____
_____

WHAT do I want?

_____
_____
_____

WHAT can I do today?

_____
_____
_____

Affirmation of the day: I AM, I CAN, I WILL, etc.

_____
_____
_____

AFFIRMATION

I WILL not let the unknown stop me from moving forward.

Repeat out loud 20 times

(For best results look at yourself in the mirror while repeating this statement.)

DAILY FULFILMENT JOURNAL

Date _/_/_

I AM grateful for…

_____
_____
_____

WHAT do I want?

_____
_____
_____

WHAT can I do today?

_____
_____
_____

Affirmation of the day: I AM, I CAN, I WILL, etc.

_____
_____
_____

AFFIRMATION

TODAY is my day.

Repeat out loud 20 times

(For best results look at yourself in the mirror while repeating this statement.)

DAILY FULFILMENT JOURNAL

Date _/_/_

I AM grateful for…

_____
_____
_____

WHAT do I want?

_____
_____
_____

WHAT can I do today?

_____
_____
_____

Affirmation of the day: I AM, I CAN, I WILL, etc.

_____
_____
_____

AFFIRMATION

I AM doing the best I can.

Repeat out loud 20 times

(For best results look at yourself in the mirror while repeating this statement.)

DAILY FULFILMENT JOURNAL

Date _/_/_

I AM grateful for…

_____
_____
_____

WHAT do I want?

_____
_____
_____

WHAT can I do today?

_____
_____
_____

Affirmation of the day: I AM, I CAN, I WILL, etc.

_____
_____
_____

AFFIRMATION

I BEIEVE in me.

Repeat out loud 20 times

(For best results look at yourself in the mirror while repeating this statement.)

DAILY FULFILMENT JOURNAL

Date _/_/_

I AM grateful for…
_____
_____
_____

WHAT do I want?
_____
_____
_____

WHAT can I do today?
_____
_____
_____

Affirmation of the day: I AM, I CAN, I WILL, etc.
_____
_____
_____

AFFIRMATION

I AM more than a conqueror.

Repeat out loud 20 times

(For best results look at yourself in the mirror while repeating this statement.)

DAILY FULFILMENT JOURNAL

Date _/_/_

I AM grateful for...

_____
_____
_____

WHAT do I want?

_____
_____
_____

WHAT can I do today?

_____
_____
_____

Affirmation of the day: I AM, I CAN, I WILL, etc.

_____
_____
_____

AFFIRMATION

I HAVE creative energy that leads me to solutions.

Repeat out loud 20 times

(For best results look at yourself in the mirror while repeating this statement.)

DAILY FULFILMENT JOURNAL

Date _/_/_

I AM grateful for…

_____
_____
_____

WHAT do I want?

_____
_____
_____

WHAT can I do today?

_____
_____
_____

Affirmation of the day: I AM, I CAN, I WILL, etc.

_____
_____
_____

AFFIRMATION

I HAVE no limits to my happiness.

Repeat out loud 20 times

(For best results look at yourself in the mirror while repeating this statement.)

DAILY FULFILMENT JOURNAL

Date _/_/_

I AM grateful for…

_____
_____
_____

WHAT do I want?

_____
_____
_____

WHAT can I do today?

_____
_____
_____

Affirmation of the day: I AM, I CAN, I WILL, etc.

_____
_____
_____

AFFIRMATION

THERE are no limits to what I can do.

Repeat out loud 20 times

(For best results look at yourself in the mirror while repeating this statement.)

DAILY FULFILMENT JOURNAL

Date _/_/_

I AM grateful for…

_____
_____
_____

WHAT do I want?

_____
_____
_____

WHAT can I do today?

_____
_____
_____

Affirmation of the day: I AM, I CAN, I WILL, etc.

_____
_____
_____

AFFIRMATION

MY dreams are real and attainable.

Repeat out loud 20 times

(For best results look at yourself in the mirror while repeating this statement.)

DAILY FULFILMENT JOURNAL

Date _/_/_

I AM grateful for…

_____
_____
_____

WHAT do I want?

_____
_____
_____

WHAT can I do today?

_____
_____
_____

Affirmation of the day: I AM, I CAN, I WILL, etc.

_____
_____
_____

AFFIRMATION

EVERYTHING that is happening right now is working in my favor.

Repeat out loud 20 times

(For best results look at yourself in the mirror while repeating this statement.)

DAILY FULFILMENT JOURNAL

Date _/_/_

I AM grateful for…

_____
_____
_____

WHAT do I want?

_____
_____
_____

WHAT can I do today?

_____
_____
_____

Affirmation of the day: I AM, I CAN, I WILL, etc.

_____
_____
_____

AFFIRMATION

I AM proud of my growth.

Repeat out loud 20 times

(For best results look at yourself in the mirror while repeating this statement.)

DAILY FULFILMENT JOURNAL

Date _/_/_

I AM grateful for…

_____
_____
_____

WHAT do I want?

_____
_____
_____

WHAT can I do today?

_____
_____
_____

Affirmation of the day: I AM, I CAN, I WILL, etc.

_____
_____
_____

AFFIRMATION

WHAT I do today will manifest success for my life.

Repeat out loud 20 times

(For best results look at yourself in the mirror while repeating this statement.)

DAILY FULFILMENT JOURNAL

Date _/_/_

I AM grateful for…
_____
_____
_____

WHAT do I want?
_____
_____
_____

WHAT can I do today?
_____
_____
_____

Affirmation of the day: I AM, I CAN, I WILL, etc.
_____
_____
_____

AFFIRMATION

I AM becoming more confident each day.

Repeat out loud 20 times

(For best results look at yourself in the mirror while repeating this statement.)

DAILY FULFILMENT JOURNAL

Date _/_/_

I AM grateful for…

_____
_____
_____

WHAT do I want?

_____
_____
_____

WHAT can I do today?

_____
_____
_____

Affirmation of the day: I AM, I CAN, I WILL, etc.

_____
_____
_____

AFFIRMATION

I AM enjoying my life.

Repeat out loud 20 times

(For best results look at yourself in the mirror while repeating this statement.)

DAILY FULFILMENT JOURNAL

Date _/_/_

I AM grateful for...

_____
_____
_____

WHAT do I want?

_____
_____
_____

WHAT can I do today?

_____
_____
_____

Affirmation of the day: I AM, I CAN, I WILL, etc.

_____
_____
_____

AFFIRMATION

I AM embracing my unique journey.

Repeat out loud 20 times

(For best results look at yourself in the mirror while repeating this statement.)

DAILY FULFILMENT JOURNAL

Date _/_/_

I AM grateful for…
_____
_____
_____

WHAT do I want?
_____
_____
_____

WHAT can I do today?
_____
_____
_____

Affirmation of the day: I AM, I CAN, I WILL, etc.
_____
_____

AFFIRMATION LIST

1. I AM THE SHIT
2. I AM ATTRACTING WHAT I DESERVE
3. I HAVE EVERYTHING I NEED TO BE HAPPY
4. I LOVE MYSELF COMPLETELY
5. I AM SUCCEEDING IN MY LIFE
6. I WILL NOT LOSE TODAY
7. I AM CONFIDENT IN MYSELF AND MY ABILITIES
8. I AM RIGHT WHERE I AM SUPPOSED TO BE
9. I AM PRESENT TO RECEIVE POSITIVE BLESSINGS
10. I AM IN COMMAND OF MY LIFE
11. I AM VALUABLE
12. I AM THE DIRECTOR OF MY MOVIE
13. I HAVE AN ABUNDANCE OF OPPORTUNITIES IN FRONT OF ME
14. I AM IN CONTROL OF MY SURROUNDINGS
15. I RELEASE ALL DOUBT FROM MY MIND
16. I CAN DO THIS TODAY
17. I AM ENOUGH
18. I AM NOT DONE AND MY LIFE IS JUST BEGINNING
19. I RELEASE ALL NEGATIVE ENERGY FROM AROUND ME
20. I AM ATTRACTING POSITIVE ENERGY

21. I AM A POSITIVE PERSON
22. I WILL STAY POSITIVE IN THE FACE OF ADVERSITY
23. I WILL NOT OVERREACT TO THINGS I CAN NOT CHANGE
24. I AM HAPPY
25. I AM WINNING TODAY
26. I AM CLOSER TO MY DREAMS TODAY
27. I RELEASE ALL SELF-SABOTAGING THOUGHTS
28. I AM SURE OF MY DECISIONS
29. I FEEL ATTRACTIVE
30. I HAVE A BEAUTIFUL SOUL
31. I AM WORTHY OF LOVE
32. I AM CHARISMATIC
33. I ONLY SEE SOLUTIONS, NOT PROBLEMS
34. I WILL BE CLEAR AND DIRECT WITH MY INTENTIONS
35. I AM RESPONSIBLE FOR MY LIFE

36. I HAVE THE POWER TO CHANGE MY HABITS
37. TODAY I RELEASE MY BAD HABITS AND REPLACE THEM WITH NEW POSITIVE HABITS
38. I AM WORTHY OF THE BEST THINGS IN LIFE, AND I ACCEPT THEM NOW
39. I RELEASE THE NEGATIVE THINGS THAT I CAN NOT CHANGE

40. I WILL NOT DWELL ON MY PAST
41. I FEEL GOOD AND HEALTHY
42. I HAVE A HEALTHY IMMUNE SYSTEM
43. I KNOW I AM MAKING PROGRESS DAILY
44. NOTHING AND NO ONE CAN HOLD ME BACK
45. I AM AN UNSTOPPABLE FORCE
46. NOTHING AND NO ONE CAN STEAL MY JOY
47. EVERYTHING'S GON' BE OKAY
48. I HAVE BEEN DIVINELY ORDERED TO BE GREAT
49. I ACCEPT ME FOR WHO I AM
50. I RELEASE ANY RESENTMENT I HAVE EVER HAD
51. I RELEASE ALL SADNESS FROM MY BODY
52. I CHOOSE TO BE MY BEST SELF WHILE I AM ALONE
53. I AM RESILIENT
54. I KNOW MONEY WILL COME TO ME IN EASY, CONSISTENT, AND UNEXPECTED WAYS
55. I WILL NOT LET MONEY DEFINE MY HAPPINESS
56. MY MIND IS IN TUNE WITH MY BODY
57. I AM STRONG
58. I CHOOSE TO RELY ON MY OWN JUDGMENT
59. I TRUST MY INTUITION
60. I WILL NOT LET FEAR EXIST IN MY LIFE
61. MY EXISTENCE IN THIS WORLD WILL MAKE AN IMPACT

62. I WILL NOT BELIEVE THE LIE THAT "I CAN'T"
63. I HAVE NO DOUBTS ABOUT MY FUTURE
64. MY AUTHENTIC SELF WILL ATTRACT SUCCESS
65. MY JOURNEY IS UNIQUE TO ME AND ONLY I CONTROL MY OUTCOMES
66. I CAN DO ANYTHING THAT I BELIEVE IN
67. I AM A STEP CLOSER TO WHO I AM DESTINED TO BE
68. MY DESTINATION IN LIFE IS GREATER THAN WHAT I CAN IMAGINE

69. I WILL ACHIEVE THE GOALS I SET FOR MYSELF
70. I AM GOD'S MASTERPIECE
71. I WILL NOT BE COMPLACENT
72. I WILL NOT LET OTHER PEOPLE DICTATE MY FUTURE
73. I WILL NOT LET OTHER PEOPLE CONTROL MY TALENTS
74. I WILL NOT ALLOW THE ACTIONS OF OTHERS TO DEFINE HOW I VIEW MYSELF
75. NO ONE CAN TAKE AWAY WHAT IS MEANT FOR ME
76. MY PRESENCE WILL BE FELT
77. I AM FOCUSED ON BECOMING MY BEST SELF
78. I AM MOTIVATED TO GO GET WHAT I DESIRE
79. I WILL DO WHAT I HAVE TO DO TODAY
80. I AM DIFFERENT, AND I AM OK WITH THAT

81. MY THOUGHTS ARE WHAT MAKE ME SPECIAL
82. I AM GENUINELY BLESSED
83. I AM WORTH IT
84. I WILL RECEIVE MY RESPECT
85. I AM FEARLESS
86. I WILL NOT LET THE UNKNOWN STOP ME FROM MOVING FORWARD
87. TODAY IS MY DAY
88. I AM DOING THE BEST I CAN
89. I BEIEVE IN ME
90. I AM MORE THAN A CONQUEROR
91. I HAVE CREATIVE ENERGY THAT LEADS ME TO SOLUTIONS
92. I HAVE NO LIMITS TO MY HAPPINESS
93. THERE ARE NO LIMITS TO WHAT I CAN DO
94. MY DREAMS ARE REAL AND ATTAINABLE
95. EVERYTHING THAT IS HAPPENING RIGHT NOW IS WORKING IN MY FAVOR
96. I AM PROUD OF MY GROWTH
97. WHAT I DO TODAY WILL MANIFEST SUCCESS FOR MY LIFE
98. I AM BECOMING MORE CONFIDENT EACH DAY
99. I AM ENJOYING MY LIFE
100. I AM EMBRACING MY UNIQUE JOURNEY

You are the SHIT!

And don't you forget.

www.ingramcontent.com/pod-product-compliance
Lightning Source LLC
Chambersburg PA
CBHW031242290426
44109CB00012B/401